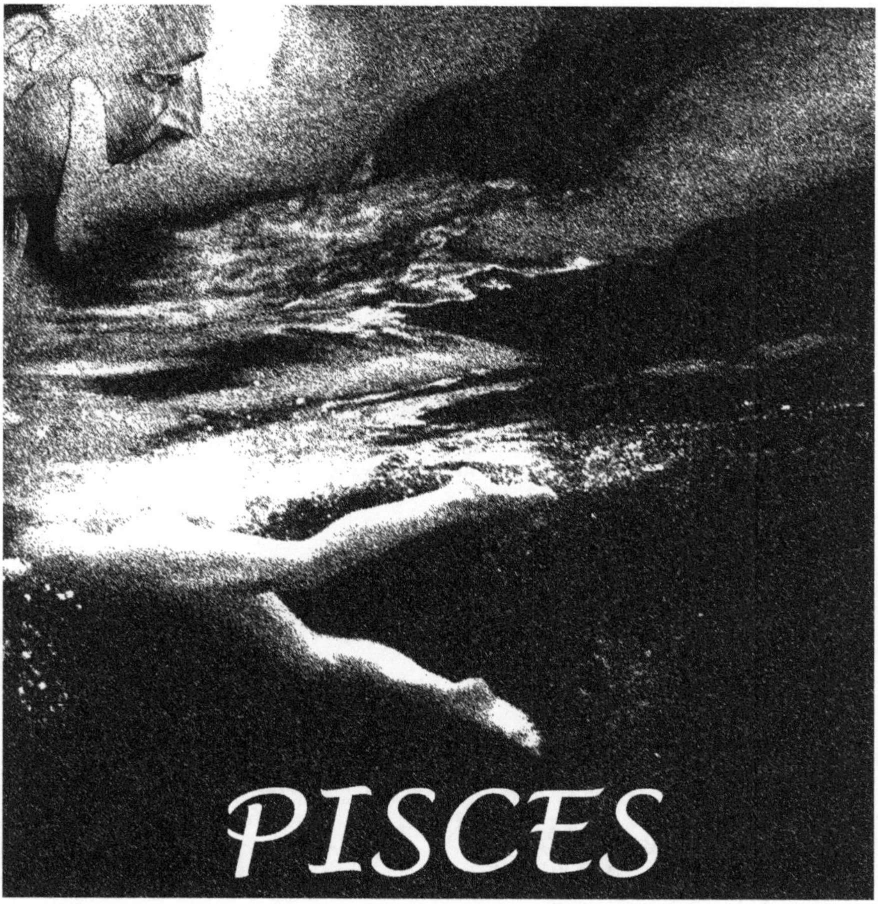

PISCES

Andrey Gritsman

SAN RAFAEL, CALIFORNIA

Text Copyright © 2007 by Andrey Gritsman

All rights reserved. No part of this book may be reproduced in any form or by any electronic or mechanical means, including information storage and retrieval systems without permission in writing from the publisher, except by a reviewer who may quote brief passages in a review.

First Edition
ISBN-13: 978-0-9753615-2-8
ISBN-10: 0-9753615-2-X

PISCES

Library of Congress Control Number: 2007938660

A *Vox Novus* Book
Published by NUMINA PRESS
www.numinapress.com

Author portrait © *by Alexander Zabrin*
Illustrations © *by YANVIK Design*

Printed in U.S.A.

ABOUT THE AUTHOR

A native of Moscow, Andrey Gritsman immigrated to the United States in 1981. He is a physician, a poet and an essayist. He has published five volumes of poetry in Russian, has been nominated for the Pushcart Prize in 2005, 2006 and 2007 and also has been shortlisted for the PEN American Center Biennial Osterweil Poetry Award. His poems, essays, and short stories in English have appeared or are forthcoming in more than 60 literary journals. He runs the popular *Intercultural Poetry Series* at the Cornelia Street Café in New York City, and edits an international bilingual online poetry magazine, *www.interpoezia.net*. He lives in Manhattan.

TABLE OF CONTENTS

PHOTOGRAPH ... 1
A DARK ROOM ... 2
TIMELINE ... 5
ONE DAY ... 6
CATCHER ... 8
WHEN WE ARE OLD ... 10
SNOWFALL ... 13
REVISITING THE CITY ... 14
ONE DAY WE'LL GO ... 17
BACKYARD ... 18
NEIGHBORHOOD WALK ... 21
YOUR SKIN ... 22
TALKING TO MYSELF ... 24
EXCERPTS FROM LETTERS ... 30
SHE ... 33
RETURN ... 34
NUMBERS ... 37
LAS VEGAS ... 38
UNBORN ... 41
A VISIT ... 42
GATHERING STONES ... 45
PERSONAL CHEMISTRY ... 46
HOPE ... 49
DEPARTURE ... 50
THE SYNTAX OF NIGHT ... 52
SEVEN CARDS ... 54
POSITANO ... 56
PAUL BOWLES. 1999 ... 59
LOVE LETTER ... 60

EYE CONTACT	63
COLOSSEUM	64
FREQUENT FLYER	67
WILDERNESS	68
ON THE WAY HOME	71
THE CITY	72
TRIANGLE	75
THREE LINES	76
SOUL BIKING	79
ROUTE 1	80
PLYMOUTH BRETHREN	83
LAST JUNCTION	84
YOU AND I	87
DOMESTIC PAGANISM	88

PISCES

PHOTOGRAPH

A landscape lives in the landscape
inside its own expectation.
And as you open the box and press,
a little bird flies out twice,
enlarged three times
during one session. Like our hope:
on a flickering Kuindzhi meadow
in his semitransparent night,
three limes reflected in the window
then sealed inside.

Andrey Gritsman

A DARK ROOM

I look into the window:
the room is dark, only the center
is dimly lit, some soft,
flickering object sits
on the square table, and
who knows what is
left unseen in the dark corners.

The room absorbs the light
from the twilight street,
from warm windows
of the other houses, from
a passerby's heart, although
the only passerby is me.

I am standing outside,
watching through the window
the object on the table.
My strained eyes see it
as a flower, blossoming,
withering, turning into an old photograph
of a man. He looks from the picture
straight into my eyes.

PISCES

Andrey Gritsman

TIMELINE

When I came here
the postal stamp cost 20c,
Pabst Blue Ribbon 6-pack - $1.49
and one antiquated bar in rural Maryland
was still hiding
the segregated areas sign
in a dark smoky corner.
In general, in those times
I was looking for love,
not realizing that I already had it.
Nothing new, business as usual,
not so bad, actually:

The clouds are coming in
and out and the dew
is vanishingly beautiful
on the windshield of my Jeep
in the morning.
And when the tree branches
rap on the glass
they remind me of multitudinous
tentacles still connecting
the neuropile of life
with the silent
underground roots
of dead winter grass.

Andrey Gritsman

ONE DAY

That's how we met:
a fluttering of letters, a fluctuation
of doubt, a heartbeat of departure.
Warm water and lavender soap
flowed down
along the beautiful engorged veins,
the bilateral malleoli and the promontory,
and then transforming into foam
that covered our feet it flew back
to childhood.

Then it was time to go
back to our lives,
suspended elsewhere
and to withdraw your hand
from mine, while your skin,
a sheath of our past,
was holding on, caressing,
feeding on my warmth,
until it would be time to pull
the last "Marlboro"
for both of us and return
to the empty shells,
waiting for us
since yesterday.

PISCES

Andrey Gritsman

CATCHER

for D.D.

You are a catcher of lights
from your childhood in the apple orchard,
a lone patrol with smokes,
a reconnaissance detachment.

PISCES

In the afternoon, after the pill wears off
your eyes are alert and out there
they are all waiting
to be taken into custody,
into account, to pay their dues of warmth,
to attach themselves to the pulsating surface,
when the announcement of despair is in the air,
unanswered calls, a fugue of fear.

Restless creature, lost between
destination points of the East Coast:
departure-arrival-feast-departure-end again,
in fact, not having any destination, leaving traces
on the highways between the streaming trees,
and in the cities, where the weathered statues
are left behind, abandoned spirits,
that outlived all parting,
not seeing you, still seeing you.

They are inside the niches on the sidewalk,
hunchbacked, lit weakly by the light
spilled from kitchen windows:
egg salad for the son or late-night coffee, before
the Valium kicks in, or a glow from the living room
where a book is left open on the low table
by an ashtray filled with the Marlboro stubs,
like fingers fallen off,

those desiccated specimens of breath,
nature morte— a still life of death
in the med-school museum
closed for the summer.

Andrey Gritsman

WHEN WE ARE OLD

for E.K.

When we are old
we'll still be beautiful.
You, always incomparable,
in your silver sweater, your gray eyes
still making them envious, because they know
that they are good, but
not good enough, and as you said,
that is even worse for a woman.
As usual you will be explaining me
to myself.

I will be sitting with my book
on the cliff (Maine, California, Crimea)
feeling that sex feeds on the seaweed,
the smell of salt and on my dialogue with you.
now this book is the only liaison left
between you and me.

I know, I will be lean and gray, ironic,
(cigar and port still in my hand)
cynical and romantic
with the same boy-like interest
in my penis, that became
the scales on a warm stone,
shed gracefully
before the lizard disappeared
into a dark deep cleft.

PISCES

Andrey Gritsman

SNOWFALL

It was going to snow. The snowfall
was so imminent that when it came
it powdered the brain. For a long time
afterwards the chilling touches
of snow covered hidden convexes
of small bones, crevices and clefts.

You were waiting for me,
pretending to be asleep and I was pretending
to be aloof as you were floating
in my hands toward the end until
it was time for me to go.

I always leave
for another winter, a passenger
on a transient train of snow.
I walk down a white street
were a car has been parked by the dark house
for ages, its green Georgia license plate
looks like a memorial plaque
slowly disappearing
in the intermittent whiteness.

Andrey Gritsman

REVISITING THE CITY

We met again in this city
where you can't name a stone,
the river or the sky.
Even the reflections of bonfires
had been named but since then
have frozen.
There the specters
still kiss ladies' gloves.

City of our youth,
place of no return
and of no leaving. At midnight

I abandon the icy station,
sit in the dining car,
drinking cheap sparkling wine,
toasting to each passing
blinding light.

After we met and after I left,
we have gone on living and can think of death
as the cityscape where in my sleep
we meet in the morning
by the same statue
where I get off the train
and pass through the spacious hall
where nobody waits for anyone.

PISCES

Andrey Gritsman

PISCES

ONE DAY WE'LL GO

One day you and I will pack,
collect our checks, collectibles, dried flowers, two or
three apples, itemize our calls,
look through the bills, change the message
on the voice mail to "as soon as we return".

As for the mail box, we don't have one.
Just a cleft in the front door.
And if one forgets to shut the lid
on a winter night
the wind gusts through the mail slot
seed snow on the living room floor,
waning at the cave of the fireplace.

One day we will sever ties, close the blue curtains,
get severance pay, pay the dues, gather up
a few blues tapes.
We'll leave shadows
in the dining room unveiled,
silverware still clinking,
woven into the hum
of the almost new furnace in the basement.

One day the breath of a distant river will grow,
precipitously congealing the air,
until the planes are suspended in flight,
chimney smokes frozen, doors fossilized ajar,
the sound of trains solid, the road brittle,
the toll attendants, turned into portico statues,
their arms outstretched
collecting fare.

Andrey Gritsman

BACKYARD

I come out into the backyard.
The moon is up and the tree crowns
are moving. Everything is
in usual order: the rake,
the hydrangeas, the grill,
a heap of leaves, the graves
of mice, birds, Lepidoptera.

They are humming under
withered grass while the house
behind me is silent. Nobody
can see me planting
another loss with my eyes closed
as yet another day
departs from my childhood.

PISCES

Andrey Gritsman

NEIGHBORHOOD WALK

I walk alone at night
by other people's houses
graced by streaming lights,
hanging plants and burnt-out fireplaces.
The invisible inhabitants are reposed
at their ritual gatherings
around a galvanized screen.

I walk along the sycamores,
magnolias and ivies,
their leaves still alive
even in January's abandonment.
This is the South for me,
where even the stars are strangers in the night,
my unseen sisters and brothers,
always there.

The stony road flickers
as I walk down to a dead end
and see the trembling vaporizing halo
over the city's inferno,
a pagan feast in the valley.

I walk along the houses
full of shadows of persisting lives,
passing the smell of someone else's day,
talking to the growing black hole,
called a slow departure.

Andrey Gritsman

YOUR SKIN

Your skin with its fine hair
reminds me of childhood
when I was told that
everything is going to be all right.
Actually, it's not,
but now it does not matter.

I feel your trembling warmth
and think of death calmly.
Not because I once found you
or you found me. Everything
happened by chance.

By now if you look at me
you will only see
your own reflection in my eyes.
As for me I am always looking
into an invisible mirror.

PISCES

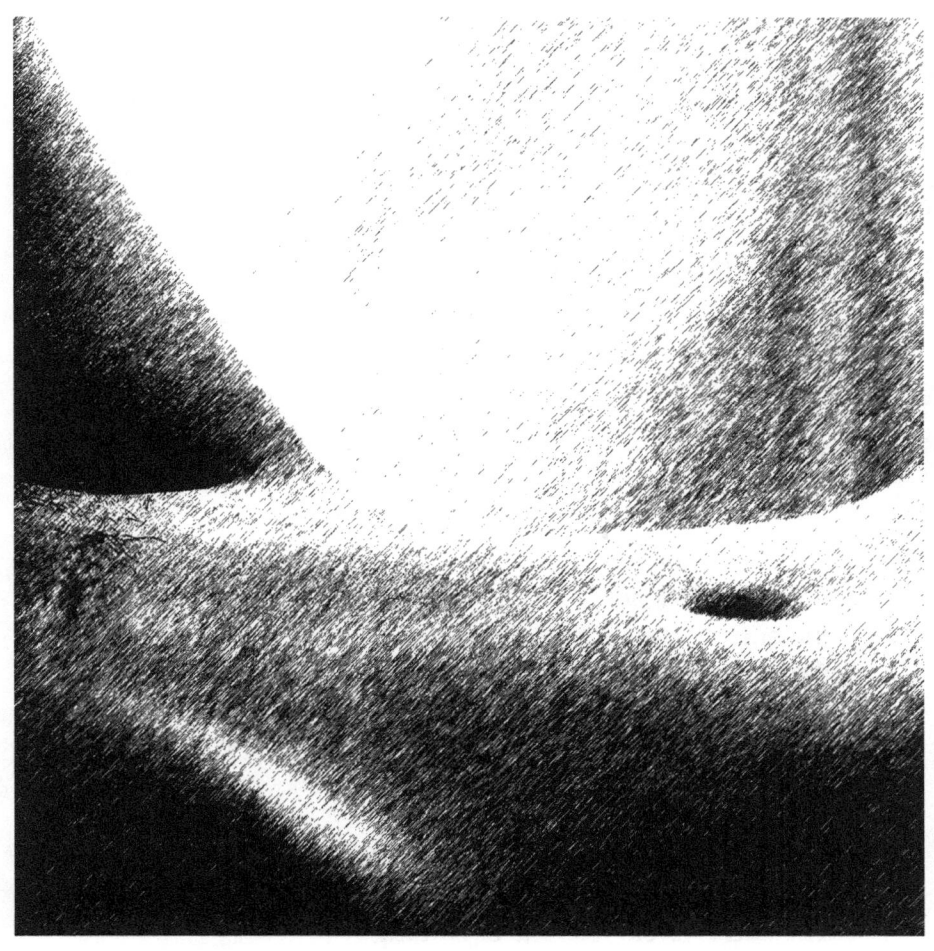

Andrey Gritsman

TALKING TO MYSELF

I open a book: birds fly out.
I close my eyes:
tulips grow in full bloom.
As life wanes, the day dawns.

* * *

Candles on the table,
shadows on the wall.
Brotherly love I've had.

* * *

Fluid souls flow from each other,
high stemmed glasses click.
The exit sign on the wall is silent.

* * *

Standing by the garden,
imagine the vowels,
the narrow consonants,
the adjectives on their tortuous roots
wavering in the sunset's breath.
Leave your hope and enter.

* * *

Bring the grains from the pyramid to light.
They sprout in silence.
The end is as close as the beginning.
So, have another one.

* * *

That is how it feels,
gliding along the plateau to the end.
Love alone drinks melting snow
in silence.

PISCES

* * *

Yesterday I saw Magritte on Fifth Avenue.
He was trying to get a glimpse of Princess Di
at Bergdorf Goodman.

* * *

I close my eyes and see with the tips of my fingers.
I feel the textures, smells and sounds,
My fingers play a silent music.

But, when I open my eyes
it's night, dark
and the usual guests have arrived.

Andrey Gritsman

* * * *TAX SEASON* * * *

There are many precipices and abysses in the mountains
of mundanity and many pieces
of the awesome and cumbersome incomprehensible
IRS-induced continuous disgraceful atrocities.

PISCES

* * *

Who knows what happens tomorrow.
The ashes from our cigarettes are still alive.
As we move from each other
we drink to all the impossibilities.

* * *

What they really want me to do
is to sell Girl Scout cookies
door to door, and still be unrecognizable.

My mistake is that I think
they all will be watching me
from behind their curtains
how I leave the block
and disappear between elms
at the end of the street.

* * *

The service of distribution of ashes
will be conducted at the chapel
in the wing B and will be televised on channel 5.
The TV terminal is available in the waiting annex
adjacent to Immaculate Conception parking.

* * *

Night is the best time of the year:
panes tremble, pines hum,
cats rustle in the bushes.

This is an open season,
the only time to get together,
to gather the stones.

Andrey Gritsman

* * *

Precision is everything -
he told me as he was leaving.

Where are you going? -
I asked him, putting my glass on the table.

Who knows, he said at the door.
* * *
You've got to be in peace with yourself -
he said emphatically.

Look who is talking, the other answered.
You'd better refocus on yourself and stop
watching other people's windows.

Then don't come walking with me at night,
see what your day was worth!
Another woman, maybe.

Come on, every time I look inside myself -
I see your hairy reflection.

Just live, OK! Don't assume anything -
he echoed.

Fuck you, guys , I said ,
while you are talking,
my life is passing by!

* * * SCUBA DIVING * * *

As I master the technique and go deeper,
I hit the bottom and spend time with the habituals:
I feel that absentminded touch
of the coelenterates, big fish
slowly approach and stare into my eyes.
I don't want to know what is behind that look.

PISCES

As I am running out of air
I feel lonesome here.
The sunrays dissipate
in the twilight of water
and only the still life: a squashed beer can,
hair-bearing condom, spent bullet shells,
make me think of home and I start up
back to the dream.

* * *

You say, that she has such unkind eyes now,
because she used to smile too much.
I say, she was born with them.

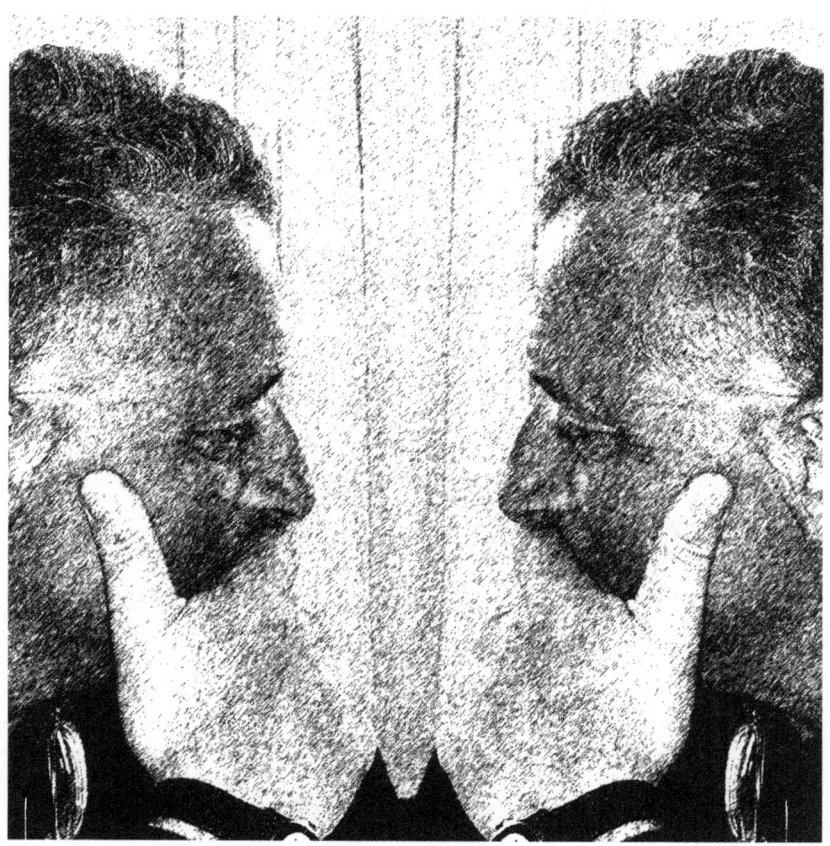

Andrey Gritsman

EXCERPTS FROM LETTERS

"This morning I arrived at school
while it was still pitch dark.
The moon was icy white
with three increasingly large circles,
a mist around it
pierced by rays of pallid light.
No poem came to me, just the thought
that you would be inspired to write
if you saw it."

"All is peaceful here.
Daniel's winter garden is producing onions,
kale, collards and soon
the garlic will be ready.
It doesn't seem like winter at all."

"I read your poems again
and can't shake the images
of the crumpled paper, the wife honking
and the sub washing up on the shore."

"See, a year later all I can think of:
levees, the bayou, swamps, an AK-47's shots
piercing the palpable humid night air,
mutilated corpses by the Starbucks'
gutted counter as in the lowlands
coffins slowly float along the batture
toward the ocean,
leaving behind
their temporary quarters."

PISCES

Andrey Gritsman

SHE

This time she comes in the morning:
lighter colors, glasses, scarf,
touches me with a veil of air
around her. She is a soft bird,
like a soul, safely unreachable.

I know her, although
I've never seen her before.
She comes every time
when I feel this.

I can't predict
what she will look like
next time. I am not even sure
whether it matters since
she will leave eventually
and may not come anymore.

I pull out a cigarette and my fingers
dart around in a futile search.
She left and took the lighter.
The darkness stands still.

I hold an unlit cigarette in my mouth;
nobody can see me
as I am trying to adjust my eyes
to being alone again.

Andrey Gritsman

RETURN

And then you'll see the same old household:
hanging plants, dark bookshelves,
the window still half-open,
a stream of autumn air,
suspended in the room,
his pen, forgotten on the floor,
three quiet paintings on the walls
(curious, cold onlookers).
The vestiges of a common life
in this corner of the Universe:
the dust, its tiny stars dancing in the late light,
small insects, a cat's world
with its own milestones,
with all those corners, smells
and hidden little sinister treasures.

The solid prewar hardwood.
The whole cocoon of another futile try.
There is no point in looking further.
They were just there.
He, by the fireplace,
always struggling with something.
This time his pipe.
She, coming down the stairs
with a letter in her light hand.

PISCES

Andrey Gritsman

NUMBERS

for A.R.

The numbers repeat themselves,
time and again returning us to a complete circle
of our lack of knowledge, back
to the graceful logic of an unending narrative.
And we still try to penetrate

the very essence of this emanating, impersonal and
absolutely centripetal passion
as we live on the outskirts of the Universe
on a clear night, lost, but not homesick,
hearing time moving, going nowhere

from nowhere. Then one can see a family
by a table lamp or by a bonfire,
the supper is over, listening to verses
uttered in any imaginable language.
The original version is running
like a shadow of a cloud
on the ruins of an ancient city by the sea shore.

A man is standing there alone
all life long, counting
unending waves.

Andrey Gritsman

LAS VEGAS

Corn on the cob.
Steak-n-eggs $1.99.
Oriental whores in tight pants.
Deodorized folks in the Venetian and the Bellagio.
Andy Warhol smiling from the sky
like a Jewish mother of nature,
ageless, androgynous.
Prostitutes' litter
on the cracked sun-blasted sidewalks
like myriads of messages in a bottle.

Mirages in the desert,
floating towards the Pacific,
condensed fluorescent magma of desire,
dirt in the surf of civilization,
vortexed into zero.

Today there is a gentle weather
and the drawings of mountains on the horizon
are almost benevolent, still living in their own time,
ambivalent towards its direction.

PISCES

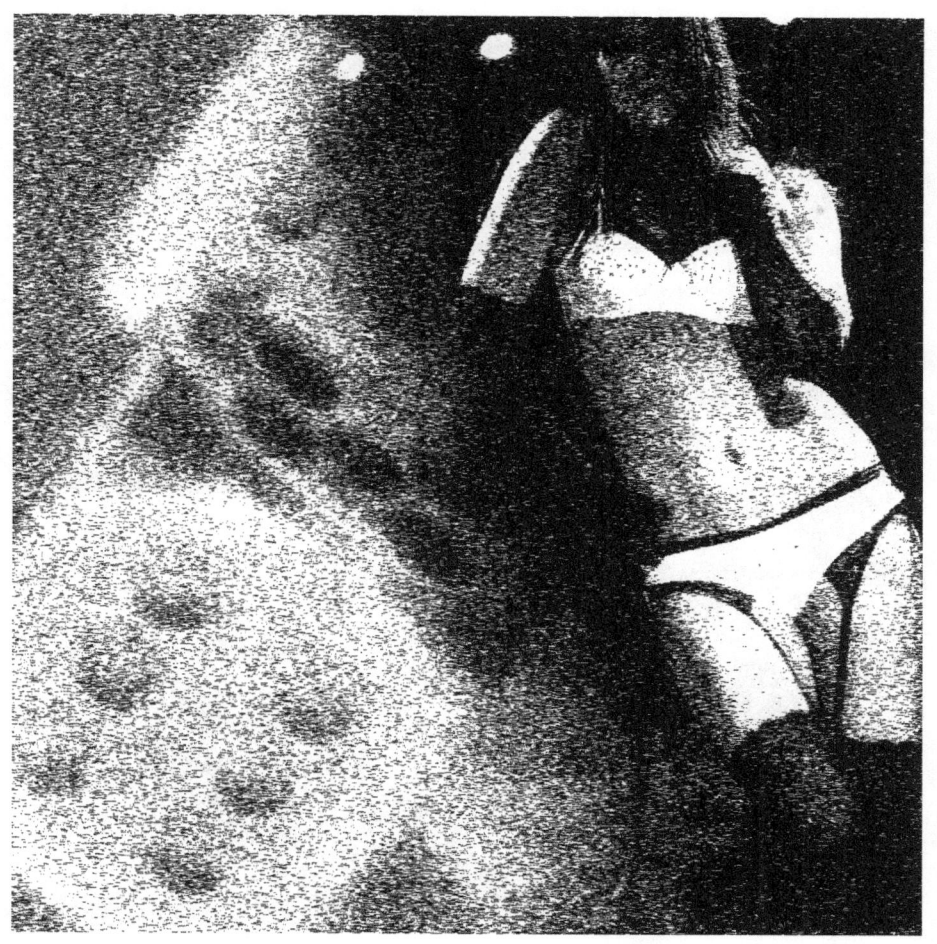

Andrey Gritsman

UNBORN

The world was glistening inside my soft universe
in the filigreed web of warmth,
pulsating and feeding my unborn hopes,
tentacles of attachments, frustrations, death.

I could have been a father, a sister,
a carpenter, a savior, a judge, an executioner.
My actuarial survival
was not yet registered.
The winds of unknowing
caressed my mother's skin.
And the pain was vanishing

because I did not exist anymore.
I was not accounted for.
And still, brothers and sisters,
we were bonded and floating together
in the shared hardship.
For only you could appreciate
my gift to you:
my silent grace, the gentle beauty, dignity
and what I would not have done to the world.

And remember, there are others
for whom not only I
but also you
are a mistake.

Andrey Gritsman

A VISIT

Going down the drain the world gargles.
Button pressed:
listening comprehension cut.

The slurred speech of freezing neon signs:
motels, convenience stores,
peep-shops. A cold train rattles along
empty warehouses. Desiccated life.
A rustle of blood-stained papers
blown away by harbor winds.

The world's surface shattered
underneath the bridge
beyond convalescence. No exit.
Anthropomorphic protrusions
on occasion are carved out
of the cloudy darkness on sidewalks.

Dive from the tangible air
of the street into the suffocating hole.
A folded bill like a snakeskin is sucked
into the slot. Curtain's up.
A rotten fish in a fluorescent aquarium
is exposed.
Only the dried-out swarms
witness the cramp of the mind's
dirt-soaked, bleeding tail.

Back to the dream safe-box:
smells cut off, noises muffled,
familiar items (from another planet)
are on the front seat,
like moon minerals, like deep-sea corals.

PISCES

A soul-saving cloud of smoke
and off you go, self-deceiving,
speeding away. No,
no, it wasn't me.
Never come back.
Until the next bout. Once
this place was someone's home.

Andrey Gritsman

GATHERING STONES

Throwing stones was easy.
Each one of them would hit a target
yet bounce off and drop and disappear
in the tall grass of the living. Leaving
was easier than we thought, because separation
meant finding someone else ready to console
and nurse somebody else's frozen limbs.

Then it was time to gather the stones,
looking attentively and inquiringly
at the withered grass, finding
some sad sequalae of previous
lives: the stones turned into cigarette butts,
teeth, lipstick, condoms, a piece of paper
with a telephone number of someone,
who does not matter any more.

Then it was time to kneel
and accept the cold condolences
of bugs, ants and dropped
dead birds.

Andrey Gritsman

PERSONAL CHEMISTRY

Every time we meet
we show each other
only a minor detail
of our real bewilderment
at a life's sentence to be carried on
as if nothing is happening
in front of our eyes.

We wear different types of glasses,
and when we switch them playfully,
I joke: what an anthropomorphic creature
you are, old man.
And you say:
I don't see you at all!

PISCES

Andrey Gritsman

PISCES

HOPE

Sounds make a song,
there is no one to sing.
It does not matter where you belong
as long as your lungs
are filled with free air.
All you know is that you've been born
alive, you are airborne
and bear vestiges of your early life
with grace: umbilical hernia,
nearsightedness, two traceable scars
on the scapulas
left from your wings.

Andrey Gritsman

DEPARTURE

This is a departure
From the original plane,
from the coast line,
escaping even memory,
asterisked destinies,
evading the estimated risk
of return on the
rest-house of life.

It's like the boarded windows
on Main Street , like an empty
cat's corner, a decimated stock
of shadows walking by.

Shadows of best friends,
loving women,
laughing acquaintances,
children leaving the nest,
lost keys.

The departure is always a chain
reaction, a farewell to everything,
but yourself,
when you eventually look inside
searching for an answer:
where the hell is he?
The news is over,
it's almost dark
and there is not much time
to be together.

PISCES

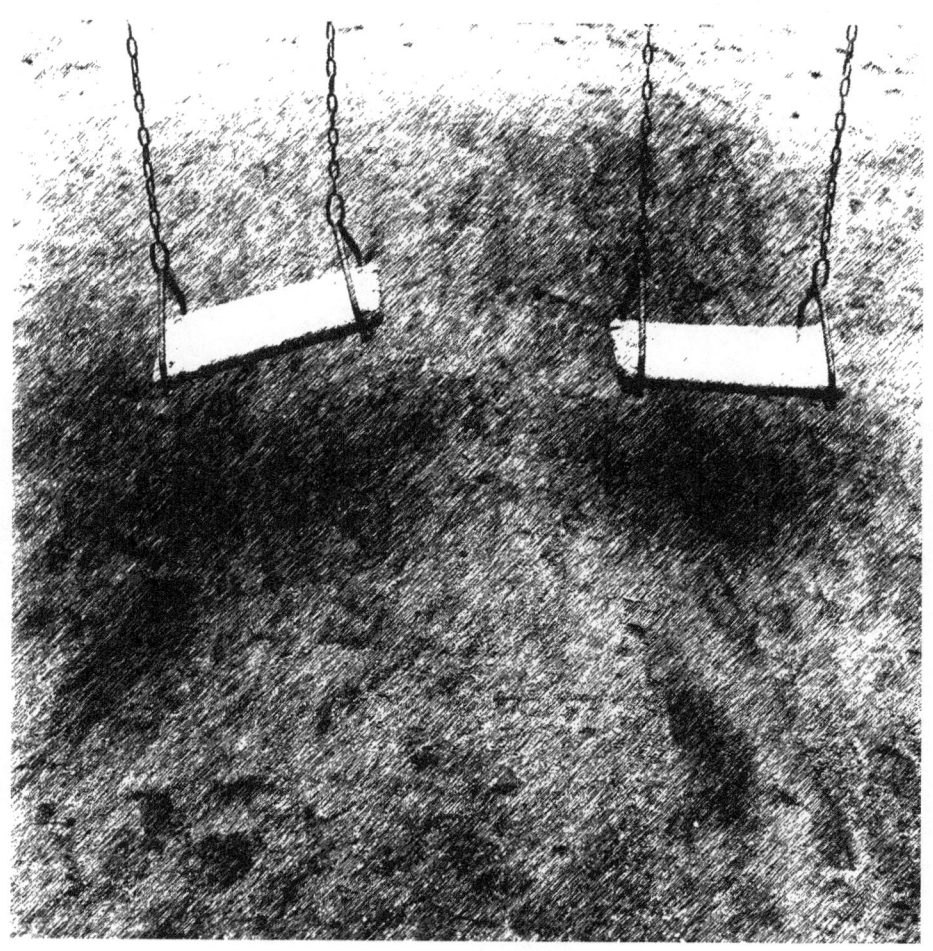

Andrey Gritsman

THE SYNTAX OF NIGHT

Listen to the sounds of disappearance:
dog barking, piece of paper
with a handwritten note
burning in the fireplace,
telephone call unanswered,
answering machine broken,
can't find your second sock,
as the wife's blowing the horn outside,

PISCES

while you're calling your mistress,
and you are set
to have a heart attack in the morning,
loving once, loving once
in a blue moon, as you feel
the sweet inkling in a Luna-park
close to the point of disembarkation,
where the stray submarine
washed up on the shore is turned
into a Russian restaurant.

There you sit and drink
to the blasting music
and sinking lights, thinking
about what you have:
those heavy stocks of an incidental life,
insuring a worthless thought of relief:
you're never alone with yourself.

These are the sounds of disappearance:
wind slowing down,
tires on the gravel,
someone's black-and-white
school photograph at the roadside
yard sale. It stares at you
before you speed away,
disappearing from its life
and then end up
sitting in your own home,
looking at the framed face on the wall,
touched by tender dust of an early Fall.

Andrey Gritsman

SEVEN CARDS

I have a box with seven cards,
my hope and the flame of my nights

The first has a window into a sunny land,
although the glass is frosted and one can't see the end.

This card is worth all other cards:
 it has the sky, stone, ice and three thousand birds.

The second card still smells of smoke
on the burnt surface it shows a block,

that can't be walked, or driven, or lived in.
It harbors the frozen breath of sky that is now crystalline.

The third card is plain, it's black-and-white,
though through a small window it shows light

above treetops and cathedral spires.
This card is almost mute, like a smoldering fire.

The fourth one tells a story that makes me smile.
It is a circus train, it is a wild

lifestyle behind a smooth veneer.
It sparkles with smirks, but leaves one with a fear.

that is indefinite. The box has a fifth card,
old and yellow, long ago cracked.

It shows the stony road, crisp night,
scents of mountain flowers, morning light

PISCES

and a woman. This is a letter that was sent
when I was born. I'll keep it till my end.

The sixth card's been played too many times.
And flows in a stream with hundreds of names.

The last card is silent. There no one can speak.
The wall is lit. Every brick

is lit by light that can't be seen but can be sensed.
The one who feels this light is blessed.

This is a letter to a floating heart.
This one is the last in the box – just an old postcard.

Andrey Gritsman

POSITANO

Mosaic Mediterranean colors:
Milk and soot.
Rectangular fragments
of stone houses scattered
on the cliff,
touched up by the moss of trees.
A spacious clay vase broken,
pieces stopped short
of falling into the sky.

Invisible scooters —
buzzing insects are born
by the cliff and disappear
into the cliff, carrying
some ones' souls
to their destinations.
From point zero
to zero: fireflies of life, smoldering
after the volcano erupted.

There is little parking here,
but John Steinbeck
did not need a parking spot.
He drank his scotch in oblivion,
good man of letters,
of one of 6,000 alphabets.
Then vanished
before it's too late,
mourning life at it's conception,
as a real poet does,
at sundown, when the first boat
departs for an unnamed island.

PISCES

Andrey Gritsman

PAUL BOWLES. 1999

Distant echo.
Soundless sand.
Breath, the homey stench of life.
The nothingness of death.
Stars stay still.
Central Park snowed-over.
A skyscraper by the park –
an overturned concert piano,
cords in elevator shafts,
souls hanging on a string.

His world is gone,
still always there.
This is the only way
for us to touch
the other side:
a snowless Christmas,
smoky verandas on the edge
of the desert.

Constant departure. The case
of torpid disappearance.
Last shot
of the century
in the rarefied air
of a personal matter.

Andrey Gritsman

LOVE LETTER

Amongst twelve voices
nursing childhood abrasions
through the lingering cautions
trying to learn separation
lying in the dark with my eyes open
making choices and breathing
the smoke coming
out of the snow-covered chimneys
eating thick beef barley
saving pills in the dark crevices
riding the last train to Poland
mourning lonely and feasting
smoking, skidding on ice, holding
on to the blind spot vainly
grasping the black box nightly
pressing all buttons at once dreaming
mumbling and singing
chasing a ghost, not seeing
you near me all my life, longing
writing by the fireplace, crossing
out and writing. All my life I am writing
an unending letter to you.

PISCES

Andrey Gritsman

EYE CONTACT

You can see that flickering
in somebody's eyes,
flared up for a moment
lasting for centuries.

Is he one of those,
who has left teeth marks
on the skulls discovered in mass
graves of the lost settlements
at the gate of the desert?
There desire was sailing
on the waves of disappearance.

It is a conundrum of what
was happening between the species
as evolution spun off
and slid into the dark, flickering
and hollow space,

into the landscape with sunburned stones,
dried blood, a spicy smell of mountain grass,
a shadow of a reposed reptile on the cliff.

These eyes are the flowers
grown in a dead end.

Andrey Gritsman

COLOSSEUM

Geometry of death.
Sun-blasted oval,
Sandblasted stone.
Stale bread,
A song of wind
Long gone
To the olive groves
Of memory.

Interlacement, entwinement
On the twilight
Of the valley.
A tourist trap by day,
Cemetery of stone
At night.

Now you know:
Salt on the soil of Carthage,
Salt beneath Masada,
Glide on sails
Toward nothingness
Of bloodhounds
Of dead Caesars
To a dead end.

Somnolent siestas
Of Italian shadows
In the courtyard:
Fresh pasta, sauce made
From an ancient recipe,
Like the sun, blasting impartially,
Blissfully, melting make-up
On the mask of the face
Of a lively tour guide
Of Berber origin.

PISCES

Andrey Gritsman

FREQUENT FLYER

for my Father

Since you've been gone
I've been flying alone back and forth
above the waters and the continents.
Both of us: me here and you there
know too well that this is a waste of time
and space.
I may fly looking for you
for the rest of my life
or death and still never see you.

Nothing can be undone,
and I can't take it.
Nor can I take the fact
that every time I see my close ones, I know,
it may be the last time I see them.

Don't worry about me. While I fly,
an angel in uniform attends me,
gives me some water and bread,
and smiles at me.
She takes care of me
until it's time to get out,
get in line for the luggage
and then to disappear into a crowd
which lives on exhaust,
cyclic persistence
and canned expectations.

The latter is something
I live on myself, expectation
melting slowly into waiting
as I keep on flying
in the space given
for the time being.

Andrey Gritsman

WILDERNESS

Three hundred yards from a ranger station by the Pacific Coast Highway, our footprints wane as we walk on the thick duff teeming with insects. A lonely lightning, a quick wildfire, and the smoldering embers leave melting patches on the dark forest floor and "goose pens" on the trunks.

A natural wooden cave inside a tree is carved gradually during two or three centuries—formerly, a shelter for an emaciated escapee from a mission, skinning a raccoon, listening to the ringtail cats that rustle in the bushes. Nowadays, it makes a cover for a gray-braided hippie, nursing his last joint, watching a mountain lion creeping after its prey or a tired hiker, listening to a heavy rain outside.

In the canyons and on the flats beside the river, sycamores marry black cottonwoods, big-leaf maples, alders, and willows. As they migrate to the south-facing slopes they give way to the chaparrals, shrubs of chamise, manzanita, and yucca. The ravines are overgrown with tan oaks, and laurels.

The cliffs remain calm, witnesses of so many ships sunk so close to their destination. At the promontory they hold the pulsating lonely eye of the lighthouse, being rather a monument to memory than a real path to salvation. The masts of the redwoods, the tallest and some of the oldest living organisms on Earth, shield the vast approaches to a hilly terrain and to the valley entrances standing on eternal guard even before God was born, when only his soul was listening in its sleep to a primordial song of the trees' tidal breathing.

PISCES

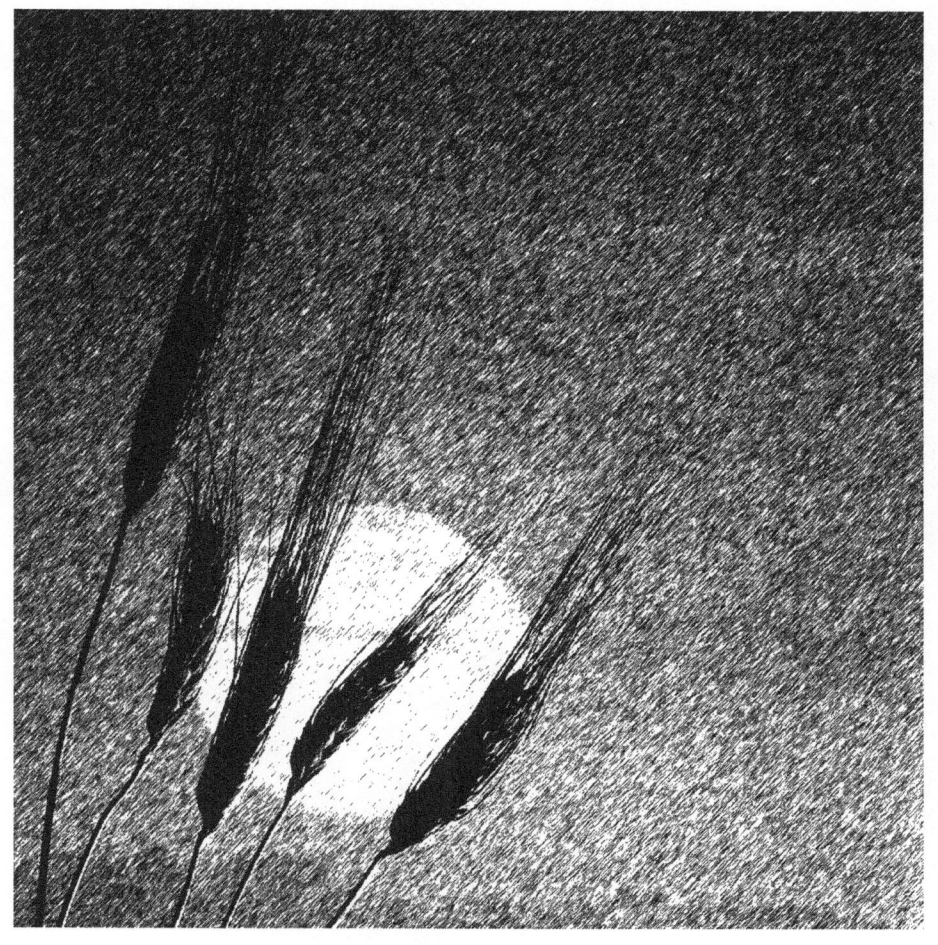

Andrey Gritsman

PISCES

ON THE WAY HOME

We are standing with a group of strangers
at a predawn hour by the unpaved road waiting
for our ride. Three hours to the station.

The lake is still asleep — splash of the paddle:
A lonely fisherman adds his brushstroke
to the night's lunar landscape. I am eight, holding
hands

with both of you and the flock of wild ducks
above us is streaming away, like our destinies,
into a bottomless well of the full moon.

Andrey Gritsman

THE CITY

The night opens the book,
reads it in silence.
The only sounds: a truck's roar by the station,
a child's cry in her sleep in a white Cape Cod
cottage across the street and my own breath.

What do I have to say to you now,
alone sitting in my car,
window down, no music, cigar cold?
I will leave for you this silent night,
torn maps, a hand lotion bottle, half empty,
a pocket Thesaurus.

Our language is spoken
only in the city, rarely visible:
bell-tower, scarlet flower beds,
barbed-wire fence,
red brick school building,
tank on a pedestal
from the forgotten overseas,
home with parents asleep,
together again,
flag with a hundred butterflies
on the desolate square.

I will leave the directions
and when you get there
you will understand the language,
mine and of all those,
who have passed through the city.
There are as many tongues spoken there
as there are transients.

I light up my smoke, start the car,
put on Abbey Road,
and head for the city.

PISCES

Andrey Gritsman

TRIANGLE

I thought we'd known each other
for a long time
until I realized that memory
is a tree losing leaves in the wind
every time the season changes.

The bare branches are drawn against the sky,
and a house behind the tree becomes visible,
the windows are open, and the silhouettes
are moving around the room.

Then they leave — one after another,
and what's left is the coffee cup on the table,
a cigarette burning, a pale TV screen,
a black-and-white picture of a woman
in a bonnet on a magazine stand.

It's quiet; the only sounds come
from the outside, and the only connection remaining
between me and him is her
trace in the air, such as women leave in passing,
even when they pretend
they were never there.

Andrey Gritsman

THREE LINES

The plane crossed
a screened window.
A scar in the sky.

PISCES

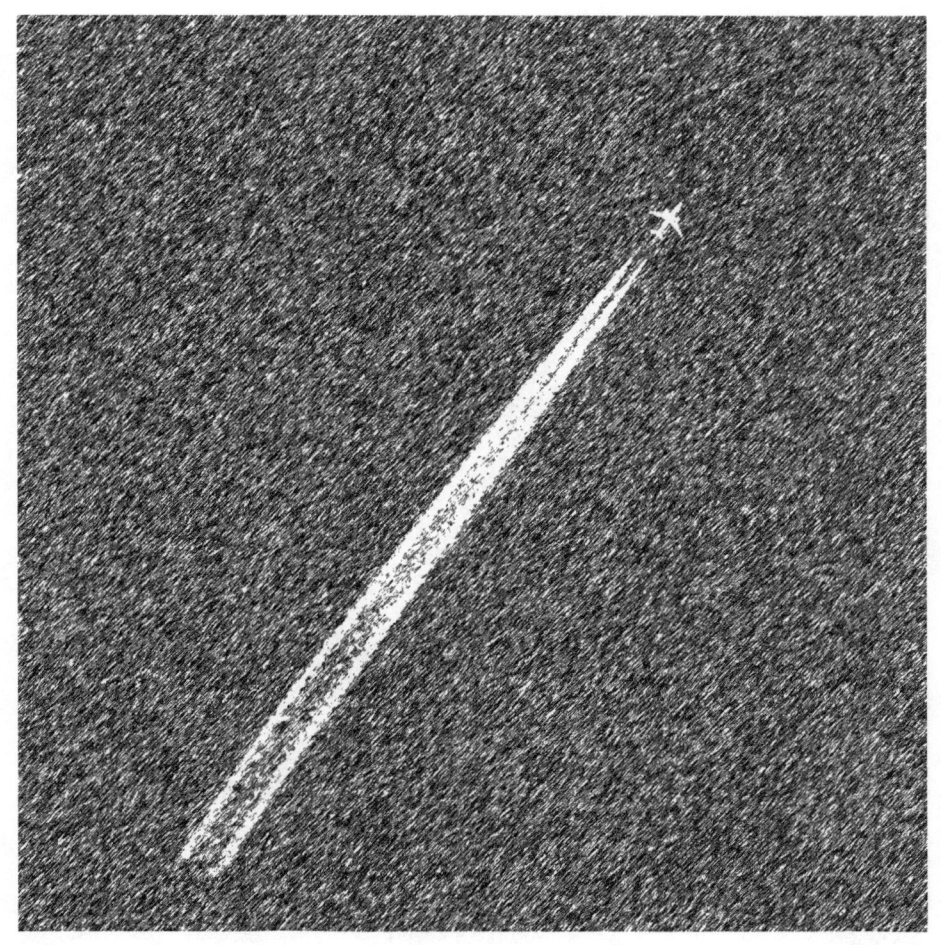

Andrey Gritsman

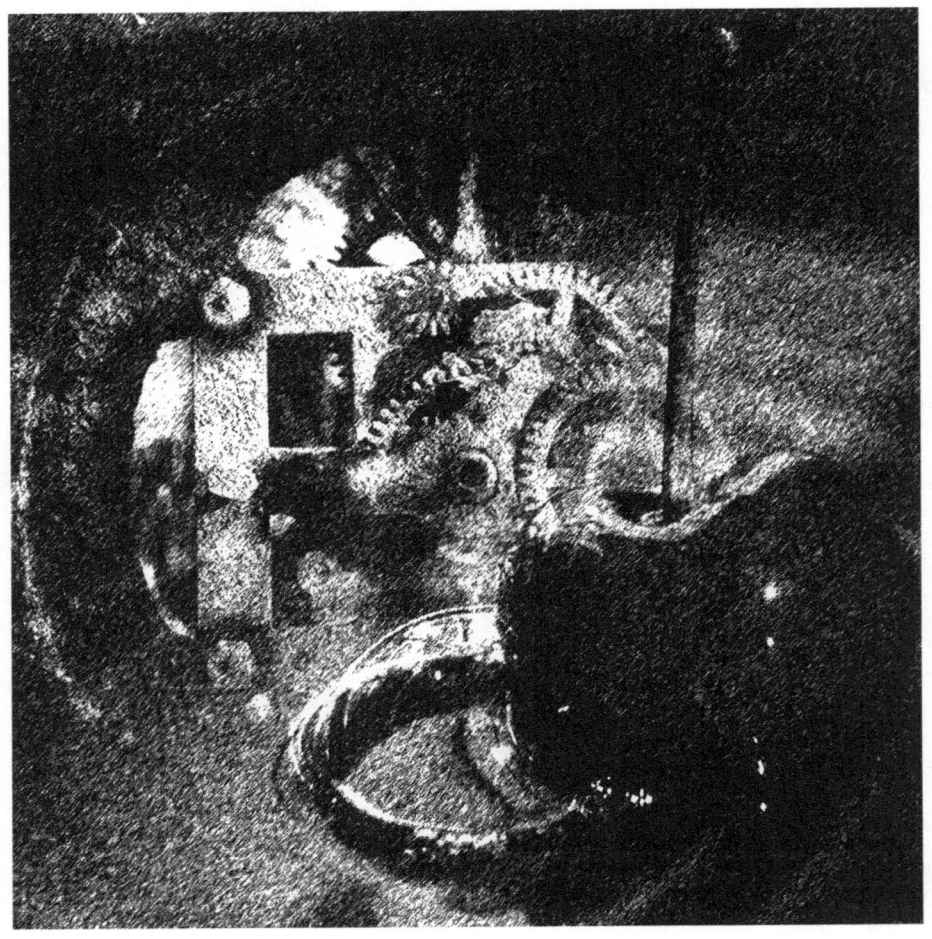

PISCES

SOUL BIKING

One sunny afternoon my soul went biking
along the river's valley into the dark ravine
of roadside chaos of the bushes and trash,
making unincidental turns
leading into the old park
in this land of youthful elders
to Pier 17, which crosses the river
midway with the view of the Great Bridge
trembling under the thousands of caskets
with many other souls sealed in them
trying to survive their movement
by not thinking.

Thinking of that my soul scanned
auburn hills, time, the paradigm of escape,
the mighty river flowing upstream,
the evolution of light, a beige trash bin on the pier,
two bikers in tight spandex,
confiding to each other
in ovulational surge.

There was nothing around
for the soul to hold on to,
except a memory
of an old shack behind the country home,
my father, his upper torso bare,
sitting under the birch tree at the dacha
resting after being on call,
filterless cigarette in his mouth,
Grandma, mourning our mutual departure,
long before it had begun,
never losing light
behind her closed eyes.

Andrey Gritsman

ROUTE 1

Route 1: warehouses, suburban barns,
abandoned shops, worn-out gas
stations, the smell of motor oil and gasoline
along the calcified arterial route
laid from the Appalachian trail
through the bifurcation of despair
along the bloodless smoldering
of the motels' perpetual vacancies.
The road dives into the green lakes
of tree crowns ever moving
on frequencies of twilight radio waves
transmitted from Atlantis to the oblivion of streets.
There, the phosphorus of sleeplessness is dormant
behind the doors: there lie with their eyes open
invisible and still DPs at night

DP: displaced person.

PISCES

Andrey Gritsman

PLYMOUTH BRETHREN

Chain-smoking, yes,
I'll have another one, thank you,
Twist my arm.
Even the band is good
in this joint for the time being.
Who are you?
Like me, a human being,
lost and found, a go-between
between the sublime and the miraculous.

We are ageless, lest we forget
a psychosomatic mutation
called love, blood, a woman
running, not in rewind,
not away from the wave
but towards the retreating,
unreachable sea, the coastline full
of broken boats: carcasses
of prehistoric animals
caught in their run, frozen in time,
suspended in space,
as the clouds gather above,
as if the Plymouth Brethren assemble
for their morning prayer.

Andrey Gritsman

LAST JUNCTION

After we part - you take East
and I take West, slow down and watch
your stop-lights waning in the dark:
crescendo-down-desperado-back again,
a precipitous inkling – incessant chasms

of nested warmth on a plain highway.
It's an exchange of secret messages,
a Morse code between two passing ships:
the Austro-Hungarian to the colonial Dutch.

And after you're gone -
it's only a message in a bottle
sent into the sea of breathless autumn fields,
transmitted mutely, the bottle

washed up on the shore, as you slow down
by a town in the land, where nobody
can understand our language
and everyone is eyeless while we live.

PISCES

Andrey Gritsman

PISCES

YOU AND I

We are on our backs in the spring grass
filled with ants, deflated condoms and
cigarette butts. Our bodies are
far apart in different parts
of the continent traversed
by the great river. Its oily sheen glistens
in the morning sun.

For a moment, we are
still together, as I watch white sails
of clouds flow between us,
reflecting the delta on a Sunday,
when the whole marina of life
is set free.

Andrey Gritsman

DOMESTIC PAGANISM

My daughter is having her Passover
at the Hillel. My son
is enjoying Easter
with his girlfriend.
They are out on a rampage:
egg-hiding, egg-hunting
and then whipping up a huge egg salad.

I answer the phone, curse, sin,
and make some money
to buy matzoh, eggs,
time, life insurance,
and to impress someone from way back,
who is not even worth it.

And God, turned into our cat,
lies dormant in the corner,
not paying any attention,
minding his own business,
waiting for the next offering.

PISCES

Previous versions of some poems in this book have appeared in other publications, namely:

Borderlands: Texas Poetry Review - "Hope"

Buckle & - "Photograph"

Cairn - "Personal Chemistry"

California Quarterly - "On the Way Home"

Carquinez Poetry Review - "Departure"

Diner - "One Day We'll Go"

Dirty Goat - "Revisiting the City"

Eclipse - "Triangle"

Hampden: Sydney Poetry Review - "Gathering Stones"

Hotel Amerika - "Dark Room"

Hubbub - "On the Way Home"

Mochila Review - "When We Are Old"

New Orleans Review - "Return"

Poetz.com - "Las Vegas," "Colosseum"

www.ingramcontent.com/pod-product-compliance
Lightning Source LLC
Chambersburg PA
CBHW051708040426
42446CB00008B/770